20
HOT PROMOTIONAL IDEAS FOR AUTHORS

*Actions you can implement
with little or no money*

Chidebere Ife Kolawole

20 Hot Promotional Ideas for Authors

© 2021 Chidebere Ife Kolawole

All rights reserved. No part of this publication may be reproduced or transmitted in any form or by any means, electronic or mechanical, including photocopying, or any information storage and retrieval system, without prior permission in writing from the publisher.

Facebook Page:
APICTS
https://fb.me/apictsworld

DEDICATION

To the Almighty God, the giver of life, hope, strength, courage and wisdom.

To every author who is working tirelessly to sell his/her book.

ACKNOWLEDGEMENT

Special thanks to my external hard disk. You broke down when I was about to export a video on *17 Promotional Ideas for Authors*. The fear of losing all my hard work made me so angry that I started writing this booklet. Eventually, you were repaired, the video was exported and a book was born.

For all the support it took to get back the hard disk to good working condition, thanks to my darling husband, Ayoola.

Jeremiah Abimbola, author of *Pianoforte*, you inspired the impromptu video in the first place. Working with you has always been dynamic! Thank you.

CONTENTS

Dedication..iii
Acknowledgement iv

One: Pre-Marketing Tasks............................ 1
Two: Promotional Ideas 3
Three: Eternal Marketing Tips................... 16

The Author 20
The Book 23

One

Pre-Marketing Tasks

Before you start marketing:

1. **Identify your niche**
   Stand for something. Be known for something. What genre does/will your writing belong to?

2. **Know your audience**
   Who are your readers? Who are the readers of your genre or topic? Where are they?

3. **Gather them somewhere or go to them**
   Either own a platform where you can meet them or register with a platform where they are. The former can be a blog,

website or brick-and-mortar reading club; while the later can be any of the popular social media platforms.

4. **Grow your audience**
   Find out what their problems are and solve them. Keep supporting them. With time, your value addition will naturally increase your audience members.

5. **Have a goal**
   Your goal can be to create awareness for your book, increase your visibility, increase your social media followers, get more subscribers to your newsletter or blog, sell a number of your books, or make an amount of money from your marketing activities. Whatever your goal is, break it down into realistic, small tasks/actions and give each task a time limit.

Two

Promotional Ideas

The actions you will take to achieve your goal can be divided into short term and long term. Note that some actions can be both short term and long term.

Short-Term Actions

1. **Bulk SMS**
   If you have been collecting phone numbers of friends, colleagues, customers, followers etc. who you think will be interested in your book, send an SMS to these people. The message should include your book title, the purchase link, and if possible a simple sentence explaining what they stand to

gain by reading the book. Some people rarely use social media, and so might miss your post about your book release. An SMS will simply remind them to go online and get your book.

2. **Bulk e-mail**

    If you have also been collecting e-mail addresses, send e-mail messages to them. Your message can be more detailed, but be careful not to bore your recipients. You can also use a service that allows you to personalize the message by using the recipient's first name. People pay more attention to something when they feel it is directed to them rather than to a group of people.

3. **Use notice boards**

    Take advantage of the notice board at your workplace. Depending on the size of the board, make a design that will be legible to passers-by. Include all the book details and the book cover, and probably your photograph. Paste the design on the notice board.

4. **Use office doors**

    If you are self-employed or have an employer who can allow you to paste a poster on doors of strategic offices, make a design containing your book details and paste them on the doors. You will not be able to tell every visitor or passer-by about your book, but that design on the door will do the publicity for you.

5. **Allow pre-orders**

    While publishing your book online, apply for a pre-order. This allows prospective readers to pre-order your book before it goes live. On the date it goes live, those people will have access to the book. A pre-order builds anticipation or interest for your book before it is released and influences sales positively. You can offer a lower price of the book during the pre-order period, just to encourage more people to buy the book.

Short-Term and Long-Term Actions

6. Seek reviews

As soon as you start making sales online or offline, kindly ask your readers for reviews. Online reviews should be posted on the platforms where the book was bought, to encourage other people to buy the book. Offline reviews should include the name/designation of the reviewer, and can be shared on your social media platforms or in other printed works to also encourage sales.

7. Write forewords

There are many people out there trying to publish their first books. Accept the offer to write a foreword for someone. End the foreword with your designation and book title/link. One of your goals is definitely to be noticed – to increase your visibility – and a foreword does that for you as people buy the writer's book. And hopefully, your increased visibility will be converted to increased sales.

8. Set e-mail signature

This is the last part of your typical letter – the part you insert 'Yours sincerely', your signature, name and designation. Whatever e-mail you use, go to the settings, find 'e-mail signature' and fill in something like this:

Chidebere Ife Kolawole,
Author, 20 Hot Promotional Ideas for Authors

Then end it with your book link.

9. Insert book details on business cards

If you intend to use a business card for any business aside your writing, insert your book details in it as well, probably on the back side.

10. Use hyperlinks

When you contribute articles online, creatively use words or phrases from/about your book that will serve as a link and take readers to a platform where your book is selling or where more information about your book can be seen.

11. Display social media handles

On the platforms where your book is selling, go to your profile; end your 'About the Author' with your social media handles, so that readers will easily connect with you, and that way, your followers will keep increasing.

12. Use publicity designs as online display picture

Get a graphics designer to make a design that will contain your book cover, book title, your name and photograph, and the purchase link of the book. Use this design as your display picture on the online platforms you are on. Make sure your designer uses the right dimensions for the different platforms, so that vital pieces of information are not cut out. For example, a 4-inch by 4-inch design fits perfectly as WhatsApp display picture.

13. Joint promotion

There are several kinds of joint promotion you can engage in with other authors. For example, you can both package your print books together at a special event and sell both at a reduced price. It makes more sense when your books share a theme with the event. You two can also publish extracts of each other's books in your books. Brainstorm! There are several things you can do with another author, especially one in your genre. You will simply be getting the attention of the other author's followers, and soon, they will follow you too.

14. Maximize marketing tools of book platforms

Different e-book retailers/distributors have different marketing tools. Go to the marketing or promotion menu under your retailer, find out the tools available and select the appropriate one based on your budget and marketing goal. Some are free promotion, countdown deal, advert on the retailer's website, custom author tab, push notification, pre-order, profile videos, social media advert, and book review that will be emailed to the retailer's subscribers. One feature that many authors do not find time to maximize is Amazon's Author Central. Go there and make the most of it.

15. Insert previous titles in current title

Do not forget to list your previous book titles in your current book. You can do so at the beginning or ending of the book. It helps to keep those books alive. Also, when a reader sees that you have published one or more books before, it builds trust and confidence in them for you. That 'amateur' label is somehow peeled off your name.

16. Insert a sample chapter of a previous title in a current title

Pick a very interesting chapter from your previous title, a chapter that can convince someone to buy the book. Then insert it probably at the ending part of your current title. It whets the reader's appetite to read more of your works.

17. Sponsor a contest or an award

If there is an existing contest or award related to your genre, become a sponsor of it. That way, your name gets mentioned during the prize-giving, or when anything important about the event is being discussed. Remember, increased visibility can be converted to increased sales. You can also create a contest/award under your genre and name it after yourself. For example, if your genre is the Christian faith; you can run an annual Bible quiz for a specific age bracket and give prizes that you can afford.

18. Use customized shirts

Make a shirt that will have in its design your book title, book cover, your name and where the book can be bought from. Be careful not to overload the shirt with too much info though. Be concise and creative. Whenever there is a big social event coming up, wear the shirt to the event. Congratulations! You have become a walking billboard.

19. Honour speaking invitations, or create a platform where you can be a speaker

Creatively or subtly mention your book as you speak. And at the end of your talk, display your book details and where it can be bought. If you have print versions, take them along to the event and display them in a conspicuous area.

20. Use a team

In all you do, never be alone. Form a team of passionate and loyal people, those who are eager to see your success. If you think well, you will find such people in your life. Share your vision with them. Prepare text, pictures and videos that contain your book details, and tell them to help you share these materials within their own space. You will go farther with a team than working on your own. Don't forget to appreciate your team in words or deeds; you can take them out for lunch or dinner.

NOTE

It is not compulsory to use all the promotional ideas here, nor do you have to apply everything you hear out there.

The list of promotional ideas is not exhausted in this booklet, definitely. My goal is simply to make you aware of the simple things you can try with little or no money.

You should make your marketing decisions based on your marketing goal, your budget, and the amount of time you can put in. Do what will be convenient for you, but be careful not to be too complacent.

Three

Eternal Marketing Tips

1. **Never end publicity**
   As long as you want to be a writer for life, publicity should never end. You must keep promoting yourself or your book even years after publishing any title. No publicity is bad publicity. Think. Use every situation, good or bad, to your advantage.

2. **Create a marketing schedule and stick to it**
   Don't just do things randomly; don't promote only when you are in a good mood. Have a timetable that will state the marketing ACTIONS to perform, the CHANNELS through which those actions

will be performed, the PERSONS who will perform the action (this is where you will appreciate having a team), and the TIME that action must be performed. After a while, evaluate your marketing strategy. Find out what is working and what is not, and make necessary changes.

Here's a template of a marketing plan you can use or tweak to your satisfaction:

MARKETING PLAN FOR ....
[INSERT BOOK TITLE]

GOAL(S): ....
....
....

S/N		PRINT	E-BOOK
1.	ACTION		
	CHANNEL		
	WHO		
	WHEN		
2.	ACTION		
	CHANNEL		
	WHO		
	WHEN		
3.	ACTION		
	CHANNEL		
	WHO		
	WHEN		
4.	ACTION		
	CHANNEL		
	WHO		
	WHEN		

* If you need a standard version or MS Word version of this template, you can make a request in the review section of this website.

3. Own a platform for meeting with your audience

Anything can happen. Don't put all your eggs in one basket. Don't rely 100 per cent on social media, distributors and publishing platforms that are not yours. Think. Create platforms online (website probably) and offline, for communicating with your audience and for selling your books. You may not have much traffic at the beginning, but you will be at rest to know that all your hard work will not be in vain should any unfavourable thing happen to those external platforms or to your accounts on them.

*To watch the impromptu video that inspired this booklet, go here:
https://youtu.be/42kbgQQbEZs
Wishing you greater sales!*

THE AUTHOR

Chidebere Ife Kolawole is the Creative Director of Ahrah Publishing and ICT Services (APICTS).

Being a voracious reader, she was a 16-time winner of the Dr D. K. Olukoya Book Quiz at the MFM Int'l Headquarters, Lagos, between Sept. 2010 and June 2013; and four of those times, she clinched the 1st prize among hundreds of participants.

Chidebere is also a versatile reader, a quality that makes editing a breeze for her. Her editing career started under the Christian genre in 2012. She is an editor and e-book publisher of notable authors like Prof. S. Ade Ojo, Amb. Albert Omotayo and Mrs Adebola Omotayo.

She has ghost-written novels and non-fiction titles; published over 100 weekly bulletin articles for The Life of God Int'l Church (LOGIC), Ogbomoso; and is the writer of 'Cashew Rush', a documentary being made by P-Cube Productions, sponsored by Anthill Studios, Lagos, with the partnership of Cocoa Research Institute of Nigeria (CRIN).

Her graphics design and video editing skills are deployed in showcasing the culture and resources of Ogbomoso through a YouTube channel and Facebook page called 'Ogbomoso TV'; she also designs and edits for Virtuous Women, an international Christian women organisation.

As a top-notch graduate of Biochemistry from Olabisi Onabanjo University, Ago-Iwoye, her love for biological science has never faded, as she spends most evenings on her medicinal garden and snailery.

Chidebere resides in Ogbomoso with her husband and son, and they live a quiet but interesting life.

She socializes on Facebook, Twitter and Instagram, using the name, 'Chidebere Ife Kolawole'; and shares educative content on the Facebook Page and YouTube channel, 'APICTS' - https://fb.me/apictsworld

THE BOOK

After publishing is done, one common concern among many authors is how to sell their books.

20 Hot Promotional Ideas for Authors equips authors with the marketing decisions to take before and after publishing is done. It lists promotional ideas that can be implemented with little or no money, with the goal of increasing the author's visibility and consequently increasing sales.

Written in a simple, direct, actionable and quick-to-read style, this booklet will definitely add to your sales arsenal.

www.ingramcontent.com/pod-product-compliance
Lightning Source LLC
Chambersburg PA
CBHW031600210526
45464CB00003B/1364